DENIM: THE F₁

CW00392876

ISBN: 978-0-9548015-8-8

CREDITS

Hub, National Centre for Craft & Design
Navigation Wharf, Sleaford
Lincolnshire, NG34 7TW, England

Copyright © The Hub 2008

ISBN: 978-0-9548015-8-8

British Library Cataloguing in Publication Data.
A catalogue record of this book is available from the British Library.
A large print version of this publication is available on request.

The Hub National Centre for Craft & Design is operated by Leisure
Connection Ltd on behalf of North Kesteven District Council.
The Hub is part funded by Arts Council England.

Compiled and collated by Phil Cosker.
Edited by Zoë Cosker
Design by Eskimo* 0114-360-9246 simon@eskimodesign.org

With many thanks to all those who sent in their words,
ideas, images and clothes – this show is for you!

CONTENTS

INTRODUCTION

In conceiving *Denim: the Fabric of Our Lives* we promised a journey: that implied a destination. In many ways our exhibition is that terminus, but in other ways it isn't. Denim means so many things to different people that it's hardly possible to say that the journey has been concluded – what's more we don't want it to come to an end. All the way through our research for this important Hub exhibition we've been asking you to send us your denim stories and pictures. As the show opens at the Hub and then goes on tour we want to go on garnering your ideas and feedback about what we have shown and the story we have told: please go on sharing your excitement.

There is something special about denim. Why, it's only a fabric? People don't, or at least not many, get really passionate about cavalry twill, Harris Tweed, brushed nylon or Sea Island cotton (we shall say nothing about leather or rubber!) but they do about denim.

As you will see denim has made various journeys since it was first used for the manufacture of garments. Many of these clothes are prosaic in function but speak volumes of the times in which they were made. We took a view at the outset that denim was a blank canvas upon which meaning(s) was created. What does denim 'mean'? The answers are as varied as the people who give them. It can signify nostalgia, rebellion, comfort, sustainability, longevity, the height of fashion, equality, value for money and innovation, to mention a few.

There are people out there who love denim; they often call themselves Denim Heads. They are denim fans: not fanatics, but people who have a vast knowledge of the fabric and an enormous enthusiasm for the garments made from it. We live, like it or not, in a society that is wedded to consumerism, where objects, once old and worn, are jettisoned without hardly a moment's regret. Aged, but still perfectly functional, objects are dumped in the nearest recycling bin (as if that action prevented waste) and replaced with something new - not something better, just new. Not so for the Denim Head. 'Wear' is as the patina on a sculpture by Hepworth, akin to the body and 'nose' of a great Bordeaux wine, as beguiling as the wisdom of old age. The more the history, and use of, for example, a pair of jeans (and it's most often jeans that are the objects of devotion) is evident in their condition the better. The way the selvedge is damaged and dirty is important, as is the way the fabric has broken down and been repaired; perhaps it's never been washed and perhaps it never should be. The garment becomes the basis of an understanding of the past but also a source of creative inspiration. From graphics to product design these 'insignificant' worn garments become iconic, representing a world where sense dictates and nonsense is abandoned. But hang on, I hear you say, that's only what denim means for them - it's not the same for the rest of us. I agree, and that's the point: denim is a canvas and as we use and wear it we imbue it with meaning. It is more than itself. It is as words are to writers: their inherent beauty and mystery always waiting to be woven into new stories.

With *Denim: the Fabric of Our Lives* we've been involved with a form of contemporary archaeology where the evidence is in our own wardrobes and memories and not in the drumlins and graves of the long departed. That is what curating the present is all about. We often miss what is before our eyes, thinking, wrongly, that what we do, what we wear, what we believe about ourselves is less important than some grand and distant history of the great and the good. Sometimes the everyday is extraordinary – such is the case with denim.

In this publication you will find academic articles as well as some of the responses we've gathered – I hope you enjoy them!

Finally I want to express my thanks to our two academic curators – Val Beattie and Pennie Alfrey from the School of Art & Design at Loughborough University – without whom this exhibition would never have come about. I would particularly like to express my gratitude to Val whom I met for the first time just after I started at the Hub three years ago who said she'd love to do an exhibition about denim – well here it is!

I would also like to thank our incredible exhibitions team lead by Melanie Kidd, who include Rachel Parker, Mia Thornton, Susanne Sklepek, Ann Worell, Alicia Butterfield and the rest of the Hub team. A special note of thanks goes to Cleo and Mark Butterfield of Vintage fashion who provided access to their extraordinary collection.

© Phil Cosker, Hub Director, 2008.

PEOPLE'S MEMORIES

"All my memories of denim are good ones. I just love denim and have done since the mid fifties when they were not called jeans but simply denim. One went and bought a pair of denims. Mind you, you were classed as a rebel and a bit of a 'scruff'." Maurice.

"My favourite denim memory was my first pair of jeans that I bought as a teenager, they were very very flared and were so tight that I had to lie on the floor to do the zip up!"

"It has to be my association of denim with rock music. Not only is denim ideal rock wear (much better than leather), it is also a canvass for badges and embroidery! Essential for 70s and 80s rock fans. My most complete denim jacket - heavily embroidered with Led Zeppelin stitching- got an airing at one of my most memorable gigs, the first Monsters of Rock Festival at Donnington Park in 1980." Peter.

"I remember making my first pair of jeans more flared by adding a "v" of different material to make them bell more from the knee down."

"My worst memory is of going on a date with a girl who suggested that I buy a denim jacket, matching jeans and black suede shoes. I bought the outfit, wore it on the second and final date and then realised that I looked ridiculous." Graham.

"My favourite denim memory is of my cousin, Karen, and I sitting in a coffee shop in my home town of Bridlington and enjoying a Coke and the kind of chat only giggly teenage girls have. It was the 70s and we were rather proud of the matching denim handbags we'd just bought. My cousin's conversation was quite animated and she was bobbing her straw in her bottle as she talked. Suddenly, the contents burst forth over the table and she grabbed her new bag to mop up the flood. End of bag. I don't know how we managed to pay and leave, we were both in hysterics with tears pouring down our cheeks." Debbie.

"In 1964 bad boys (that is cool boys) wore ice blue denim jeans and that was attractive and girls would wear short denim skirts and that was freedom/self-assurance."

"I had some skin-tight, dark blue drainpipe jeans with huge turnups. But it's the memory now that's worst - I loved them at the time. They were our going-out-to-parties best and were worn with an open neck shirt. Our hair flowed down to our collars and we danced with mum at a number of village hall events and family weddings. Viva cherryade and being able to stay up late." Simon.

"I had cheap stretch jeans when I was the wrong size to be wearing them."

"My mother found me in the bath shrinking them on; from then on she concluded I was mad." Francis.

"I bought a pair of white denim jeans which I thought were really cool at the time. The trouble was I also bought a pair of very high cork wedges to go with them and then set off to see my relations in the North East, travelling by train from Kent via London. I fell over on the way to our local station, then again 3 times in London and by the time I reached Newcastle my beautiful jeans were a mess and I was covered in bruises – so much for Miss Cool!" Denise, aged 56.

"I wasn't allowed to wear denim jeans in my teens as my mum said they were common. I think I was married before I actually got a pair. I like wearing them now though." Val, aged 64.

"In the late 50's a new shop opened in our town. Every Saturday crowds of what came to be called 'teenagers' could be seen ogling the fantastic American-style clothes filling the windows with colour. In the window a large photo of James Dean on his motorbike and dressed in his jeans, proclaimed the new era. In the window on the other side of the entrance Elvis struck a pose dressed in his Jailhouse Rock prison blues. To own a pair of Levi's was really something. So, I asked my dad if I could buy a pair. Guess what - "I don't want no juvenile delinquent living in this house" and that was the end of that. What he didn't know was every Saturday night I borrowed a pair of denim blues from my mate and off we went to the Roxy - Cool Cats Yeah!" Cliff, aged 65.

"This is a fabulous idea! I don't have any pictures to send you but can share some denim moments...since I live in India and am Indian, denim came to us in the early seventies. It hit us like a tantalizing desire, transforming our bodies when we were able to find a pair of blue jeans to wear. Most of us were dependent on relatives who went abroad to get us some....and we waited in frenzy till they returned. We sometimes wore big flared denims, but, most of the time, the classic men's type. However, local brands soon came into existence and slowly denim became a more natural part of our lives." Meera, aged 42.

"When I was growing up we had denim jeans, dungarees, jackets, coats, hats, pencil cases, bags, purses, waistcoats, dresses, skirts, shoes and boots. If it wasn't made of denim it was made to look like denim, including crockery, wrapping paper and record covers – remember the Rolling Stones 'Sticky Fingers' cover?" Mali, a 50's child.

"As a teenager I remember sitting on the bus one day (in the late sixties/early seventies) next to Sandy McKenzie who was dropping the ash from his cigarette on to his denim jeans and rubbing it in, in order to make them appear faded (or to speed up the process). They didn't sell them pre-faded or pre-shrunk in those days - you had to work hard to make it yours." Ailsa.

"When I was 15 the Indie Scene had just started. The Stone Roses, Inspiral Carpets, Carter and The Unstoppable Sex Machine and James telling us to 'Sit Down' was the only thing an Indie could listen too. The Indie'r you were the better.

To let everyone know that you were an Indie, jeans played an integral part of the uniform.

I remember writing as many band names as possible all over the jeans, followed by rips on the knees. These rips had to be carefully applied to look authentic. Too much and your knee popped through. Add to that carefully controlled splashes of bleach over the legs, my hair in a ponytail, and a Glastonbury wristband that stayed on for moths, and there you have my outfit for 1993." Andrew.

"I got my piece of denim from Oxfam in Stamford (£4.99). As I don't often wear blue, due to its association with a previous job uniform, this was a new clothing direction for me. The shirt is slightly too big, so it has that comforting 'envelope' quality, and it's put in loads of hours as an all-purpose printmaking and holiday shirt. It's indestructible, which suits me fine. I cut the collar off as soon as I'd brought it home, so it's less fussy in appearance and suits my face better. It's usually worn with sand-coloured cords or skirt; saved exclusively for daft artistic pursuits and anything involving mud, bicycles, or task-specific footwear. Speed on, supershirt!

I'd struggled for years to find an interesting pair which a) fitted round the waist as well as the leg, and b) didn't make my behind look like Nellie the Elephant in retreat. And then I faced the price problem: I couldn't stand the idea of extortionate 'image' brands or the cheap-and-nasty alternatives that never look right. So I didn't bother with jeans until I went into a Gap '75% off' sale in 2007 and found on the chap's rack a straight-leg pair with a waistband that looked about right. Yaaaay! Not only the right-sized waistband, but the right leg length too. Problem solved, after about 20 years of trying things on. They're grey rather than blue, so that helps; and the twill weave is particularly nice. In future I'll forget about the size 12-14's and go for the 30 x 30's instead. Wish I'd known earlier - I could have been almost cool, at the right age." Lynn.

"My Dad used to have this massive denim jacket, with patterned cotton lining, and way too big for any normal sized human being. It was meant to be like that though; the elasticated cuffs and general sack-like effect it created when you wore it. He'd looked very cool in it when he was my age, I'm sure. He was clearing out his wardrobe a couple of years ago and I happened to be there when he tossed the jacket in the pile 'to be disposed of' via a charity shop or just dumped. Being the curious little soul I was who had never actually worn a denim jacket before, I put it on and liked it. Sure my hands didn't even remotely reach the end, but it was big and sturdy and smelled like my Dad. He said I could keep it, and I still wear it sometimes, mainly when I have a cold, and then only in the house. It is a little old fashioned, after all. Secretly, I still love it."

"I recall that in the early seventies the only jacket to wear was a Wrangler Denim Jacket. Loads of people bought Levi Jackets but they never fitted a teenage body quite right, so they were shortened by removing the bottom welt, cutting an inch or two off the jacket and reseweing the welt back on, often very badly. But those in know wore Wrangler. Some customised them with Dylon dye or Bleach, some even embroidered them. Most turned the cuffs and the collar up which caused great annoyance to my mother, but the real style issue was that the Wrangler jacket had high mounted side pockets which, when you put your hands in the pockets, made you as look as cool as a strutting catwalk model as you walked down the street. Wrangler Jacket, Levi 501's, black converse and a collarless shirt...would it look out of place today? I was a budding musician, certain of fortune and fame - and the Wrangler Jacket confirmed it!" Wally, aged 51 (referring to 1972).

"In the 70's there were A-line skirts, constructed of gores and buttoned down the front. Jeans were dramatically flared with rounded pockets and mainly light blue. Old jeans could be used to make handbags and Blue Peter style pencil cases, in a hippy spirit of recycling. The early 80's saw coloured denim. I had some green jeans from Manchester Miss Selfridges, which were a baggy construction, joining half way down the leg, with turn-ups to emphasize the green and worn with red 'Kickers' shoes. Skirts were straight and jean shaped at the top, worn above the knee with flat loafer shoes, ankle socks and Fred Perry tops. Jean jackets were a sleeveless 'gillet' shape. Dark blue drainpipe jeans were also popular (sometimes with the need to lie on the floor to get them on!) and the inner seams could be sewn to make them even tighter fitting and tucked into short pixie boots or worn with loafers. 'Designer' jeans appeared. A friend had 'Gloria Vanderbilt' ones with logos embroidered on the pockets. Names were important, such as Lee, Levi and Wrangler. Dungarees also became fashionable and mine were light blue with a woven-in pinstripe and turn-ups, with loops for a belt, but worn loose.

Pale blue jeans were the only thing to have during the late 80's, along with the various styles of stonewash and distressed denim.

The 90's saw black jeans and different styles such as bootcut and relaxed fit. In jackets, I had a flying jacket style with an asymmetric zip fastening and zipped sleeves, worn with cropped tops. A skirt I had at the time was in dark blue with a jeans shaped top, but flaring out into panels.

The 21st century now has us back, full circle, to the 70's spirit of recycling and I am using washing machine dyes to give my old jeans a longer lifespan and harking back to my favourite 'green jean' days. I am also no longer ashamed to wear flared jeans once again, which are surprisingly flattering!"
Diane, aged 42.

"The sixties bring back memories of winkle-pickers, stilettos, mini-skirts, bobbed hair and the jeans – oh the jeans. Girls couldn't buy good fitting jeans, so we bought men's jeans. We then sat in a hot bath and waited until the water cooled to shrink them into tight trousers. We then dried them while still on and struggled to get them off, usually leaving your skin dyed the colour of the denim. Oh, those were the days, and oh to have them back. They say if you remember the 1960s, you weren't there. Believe me, I remember them well, they were fantastic and I certainly was there. It was the best decade of the twentieth century." Thelma.

"I was watching a BBC programme on 50's rock'n'roll and Stuart Machonie quoted Peter Blake saying that he couldn't buy denim jeans in the 50's in England. So in order to get the right look he had to buy dungarees and cut the bib and braces off." Mark.

"A pair of baggy jeans can give one's arse the look of a old saddle bag – hence the washing at high temperatures & tumble drying – Not good for the environment but great for my vanity! Shame on me.

A friend once told me when we were out shopping, 'always buy a size smaller in jeans'…But what happens if you can't even get you're arse into them and the zip doesn't even meet in the middle?! Hence back to my buying the right size and my laundry ritual.

Needless to say "muffin tops" just aren't attractive!" Anon.

"I come from a comfortable, cosy, middle-class background so it's not surprising (well, not to me) that my first pair of jeans came from Marks and Spencer. Probably circa 1966 or '67 and were the result of a sustained campaign of whining that eventually wore down my parents' resolve prior to a hostelling holiday in Alloa. Dark blue with massive turn ups, as I recall, and delivered with strict instructions to keep them clean.

However, the seeds of brand loyalty were sown and between those remembered beginnings and today denim has been a constant in my wardrobe. I admit I have tried the patience of Mr. Strauss and worn creations that might be better forgotten, but denim it is.

Along the way my wardrobe has been home to high waisted wide legged baggies, skin tight hipster drain pipes, Loons (a health hazard in the rain), flares, boot cut, slashed, ripped, patched, cut , tie-died, hippy and skin head. £3 from Tesco or £150 Red Flash Levis - I've worn them all.

And then there were the jackets –double dart Levis, parallel Wranglers and for a while in the late 70s a suit and a full length overcoat.

Fortunately I never succumbed to perhaps one of the worst fashion faux pas of the early 80s - denim cowboy boots.

Today my favourite denim item is a faded, battered jacket. We've grown old together. The collar and cuffs are nicely ragged and on the right arm a couple of holes are evidence of a motorbike tumble. The bike and I had parted company but the jacket kept man and machine attached as we skidded to a halt. The wing mirror sheared off when I hit the ground and the shaft pierced through the jacket's sleeve holding me to the bike. I broke my kneecap and the bike needed some surgery too.

Eventually that bike went. The jacket remained." Chris.

"I was in my late teens when my friend Pat took his own life, my first real taste of loss. I successfully bleached a Levis jacket in a bucket (past attempts had left a pile of buttons) and went to the local art school where I had one of the students screen print the cover of Spear of Destiny's single 'You'll never take me alive' on the back. It had other bits added, like a gothic tie dye collar, patches and badges. It became a shrine I wore to the gigs of the time. The Smiths, Echo & the Bunnymen, Siouxsie etc. I think it helped the healing process. I still have it to this day and would be pleased to let you use it in your exhibition." Andy.

"Denim was de-rigour for Art Schools in the sixties, when there still were art schools. Levi's, occasionally Wrangler's but it was hard to get the good ones. The Levi's were very stiff, and I mean very. Yes, we did sit in the bath with them on, and yes, they did get 'crotch' hugging tight, but I had to do it, because otherwise I would be red raw between the legs and behind the knees. Besides, I worked with stuff on the floor and it helped to be able to bend!" Roger.

"Back in the 60s and 70s I was involved in the music business in a number of different ways - as Manager, Agent and Promoter.

I discovered and managed a group who became the Beat Merchants – EMI recording artistes. Nationwide tours with Lulu, Gene Vincent, Brenda Lee, Honeycombs etc. and appearances on TV's "Thank Your Lucky Stars" and "Beat Room". I even went with them to mime a radio show...think about it!

They had minor hit records in the UK, and a No 1 million seller in the USA. Part of the marketing were Beat Merchant Shirts - on sale everywhere, including, of course, Carnaby Street. The shirts were pale blue cotton, with DENIM collar and cuffs." Cary.

"In the early 60's I was a Mod, part of the Tottenham Royal crew. We used to love Ready Steady Go which was really influential as regards new styles and fashion. There was a great buzz about Levis, and we all had to have them. At that time they were sold as workwear only. We went to a shop in Tottenham that sold boiler suits and such items for workingmen.

My friend and I were so excited by our purchases, which of course had to be shrunk to fit in the bath. I still remember how the colour came out as I sat there, and it turned my legs blue!

My auntie was quite disgusted by us wearing them as they were men's, and had fly fronts, which no women's trousers had at that time. It wasn't "nice", not the done thing. My aunt at that time was 21, but there was such a gap between us as I was 15 and she was a real grown up with different values. I think we were the first kids who had the choice never to become adults as had previous generations.

Later on, I put brass paperclips all down the side seams to give them a studded look. The paperclips were the sort that have a round stud like head, and two legs that you bend back. They were extremely uncomfortable to wear! But I guess you have to suffer for fashion." Cleo.

"Smell of denim in the Army Store, aged 7 or 8. Style Mod, mini Lambretta 200, got to wear 501s Red Tag (bigE), shrunk to fit. Like Andy said, 'nobody can get a better pair of levi's than you' (true, at the time)." Rich.

"My Wrangler Jean Jacket.

...The date is autumn 1968, I have just finished three years postgraduate study at the Royal College of Art – a great time, plenty of posturing and acting in a 'hip' fashion. Suddenly I am forced to find employment in order to support my wife and young family. I am appointed to a new ceramic post in Nottingham Polytechnic; shock horror, I had never visited the Midlands before and had no idea what to expect. T-shirts and jeans were the universal dress code of the day; in order to have good street cred, clothing was imported from the USA - Wrangler or Levi especially.

Come my first pay day, now with a very short hair-do and Doc Martin boots, I managed to buy a tight-fitting blue denim Wrangler jacket: slit side pockets, breast pockets with flaps, waist hugging and plenty of brass studs – here I was aged 28 and very much Jack-the-Lad. This jacket became an important icon to me, often posed in at concerts and dances, but rarely worn on the streets.

Alas, the introduction of good Nottingham ale, more money, rugby clubs etc. changed my early slim appearance. I carefully hung my jean jacket in my wardrobe where it has remained until today. I am told by my sons, who were never allowed to borrow it, that it is now a collectors' item, but to me it is an important reminder of a very special period in my life.

The bib and brace denims in a faded blue and soft texture played an important part in my ceramic workshop life in the mid to late '70s. I moved to the Lincoln School of Art after a few years lecturing at Nottingham Polytechnic. I was now fully engaged teaching and making my own ceramic work.

The excellent and comfortable design of the Levi overalls gave me good studio and workshop protection but also identified me as a middle-aged trendy fashion victim. Deep pockets and protective bibs were 'de rigueur', to be worn with colourful short- or long-sleeved t-shirts and, of course, coloured boots.

These denims were purchased in the Army & Navy Stores in Lincoln, a regular haunt of the art fraternity in Lincoln. They were carefully washed and eventually put away in my wardrobe as my various roles changed and I became more involved in art school management and new images had to be expressed."
Pete.

THE ORIGINS OF DENIM

It is impossible to determine exactly where the origins of denim lie; although many more recent sources have claimed that the term 'denim' is a miss-spelling of 'de nim', which is in turn a corruption of 'de Nîmes', thus indicating that it is a topological term, there is no firm evidence that denim did in fact originate either in Nîmes or even in France. To the contrary, there is strong evidence that suggests that the origins of denim lie within English textile history. Until the 19th century, France looked to England for textile manufacturing expertise. So if the origins of denim do lie within English textile history, why should an English fabric be given a foreign name? As is often the case today, it was not uncommon for manufacturers to glamorise their products by giving them an exotic image, and one way of achieving that was to name a fabric after a foreign location. Commercial nomenclature, as well as the appearance of a fabric, could be somewhat unreliable.

Serge de Nîmes, to use its full name, was one of a large family of work-wear fabrics that were widely produced throughout northern Europe and dominated by the textile sub-group known as 'serge', a silk and wool, or all wool twill (depending on the quality), that was produced as far back as the 12th century.

The Oxford English Dictionary cites two references to denim: the earliest appeared in a London publication, 'The Merchant's Magazine', in 1695, when "serge denims" were listed; and the 'London Gazette' of 1703 referred to a "pair of flower'd serge de Nim breeches". A little later, the first edition of the Encyclopedia Britannica (1771) referred to 'London serge' that was: "highly valued abroad, and of which a manufacture has been for some years carried on in France". The "manufacture" was quite possibly that started by an Englishman, John Holker, who had settled near Rouen in 1750.

The absence of standardization in terminology mirrored the inconsistencies in production, so while we cannot be sure what the term 'serge de Nim' meant, we do know that 'serge' denoted a twill woollen cloth, and that references to 'serge de Nimes', or 'de Nim', or 'denim', become more frequent from this time on, until the 19th century when 'serge de Nimes' is dropped and 'denim' becomes a common term. Nevertheless, the earlier practices of fusing one textile term with another continued to create confusion, as demonstrated by the entry in Webster's American Dictionary (1913) in which denim is defined as: "a coarse cotton drilling used for overalls", implying that denim and drilling were interchangeable terms. 'Dungaree', derived from Hindi to mean a type of Indian cotton, represents a merger of a textile term with a garment term, to arrive at the composite meaning of work-wear trousers with bib manufactured in denim. 'Jean', 'Jeans', 'lining jeans' and 'Jeans Fustian' ('jean' was a corruption of the English name for Genoa) began as a woollen or mixed fibre fabric but, like serge de Nîmes, evolved into an all cotton fabric - although the Indian Textile Journal of 1897 defined 'jean' as a plain or striped wool and cotton mix, while the Encyclopaedia Britannia (1911) defined it as: "a variety of heavy woven fabrics, chiefly...for men's wear". Drill, drilling, drugget, fustian and drabbet, on the other hand, were purely textile terms that had no associations with garments but denoted hard-wearing, work-wear fabrics that featured a similar or identical twill weave structure to that of denim, jean and serge.

What can be gleaned from a survey of the development of textile terminology is that textile terms were often used unreliably; that the textile trade had long been an international one with much cross-fertilization; and that textile terminology often side-tracked the origins of a textile in order to prioritize other factors such as weaving methods, raw materials and style.

There are two main features that determine the success of a work-wear fabric – the strength of the fibres and the strength of the structure of the weave. By the 18th century, Manchester had established itself as an important centre for textile technology and innovation where a wide range of durable fabrics, that included fustian and 'lining jeans', were manufactured. Cotton began to replace wool as the mainstay of work-wear fabrics, although a wool/cotton mix was also a popular choice.

These developments were mirrored in America, where George Washington toured a textile mill that wove both jean and denim in 1789, and 3 years later, in 1792, 'The Weavers Draft Book and Clothiers Assistant' illustrated a variety of denims, accompanied by technical instruction for their manufacture. By 1848 the American artist, Richard Caton Woodville used denim as an indicator of lowly status in his painting 'War News from Mexico' (1848, National Gallery of Art, Washington). The portrayal of a black labourer dressed in a red smock with patched blue denim jeans, described as "ridiculously good" in a contemporary review of the work, is in stark contrast to the gathering of soberly-dressed white men positioned on the step above him. Although this work cannot be entirely interpreted as social realism, Woodville used blue denim jeans as a sartorial sign of black slavery in early 19th century America.

By the date of this painting, Amoskeag Mills, in Manchester, New Hampshire (the place name was changed in homage to Manchester, England) had established a high reputation for the quality of its all-cotton denim, duck, drill and ticking materials, thus confirming the significant similarities between these fabric types. The Amoskeag Mills attracted valuable customers such as Levis, but also unwanted imitators; thus, in 1879, they sued a ticking manufacturer who fraudulently used the Levi trademark (again, this locates denim in that family of common fabrics that includes ticking). However, by the end of the 19th century the quality of Amoskeag denim could not compete against the increased competition from denim mills in the southern states, and they consequently lost their Levis contract to Cone Mills, who had been established in North Carolina since 1891.

Colour is also a critical component of denim's identity. A wide range of colours appears to have been available since the 17th century that included brown, black, olive, buff and white, but by the 20th century indigo blue had become dominant. Once denim hit the high fashion stakes in the late 20th century, the palette widened to include yellow, red, pink, purple, green and grey, and blends with other materials including lustre effects created by metallic or nano-particles introduce yet another visual dimension. But, for most people, the most prominent characteristic of denim is its indigo-coloured warp/white weft profile that, in apparel, results in the unique unevenness of wear that maps the personal profiles of interactivity between the wearer and his/her environment.

This unique relationship between the fabric and the wearer has inspired a range of highly creative advertising imagery that has exploited the symbiotic dynamic that suggests a fusion between denim and the body, so that denim becomes an extension of the physical and non-physical self.

Modern denim is the product of a complex process of change and diversity in its evolution and the modern usage of the term 'denim' encompasses that diversity. Thus the story of denim is easier to understand if it is viewed not as one textile, but as a family of textiles in which members are connected by certain common features that also accommodate difference, including new mixed fibres and colours. It is the story of endless experimentation, through spinning and weaving technology, which is why denim cannot be defined simply. Denim is a textile that has been evolving for over 300 years, and continues to evolve whilst retaining strong links with a past that ideologically contributes, at least in part, to its enduring appeal. Today the main producers of denim are located neither in England, nor in the USA which had come to dominate denim in the 20th century, but in Asia and the Far East.

Modern denim and its defining features

The main characteristic of denim is its warp-faced twill construction – it is this that gives it its strength, but also its ability to mould itself to the wearer's form, taking on an impress of the body within. Similarly, jean and drill are both warp-faced twills; thus the distinction between denim, jean and drill has become eroded and the terms are largely interchangeable. Historically both denim and jean were given different sub-group names, such as "dice" or "balloon" denim and "fancy mixt" jean which may have indicated either structural features, and "New Creek Blues" which may have described a particular quality of blue. Although the most popular colour for denim today is blue, it also comes in an even wider range of colours than ever before, from white, grey, black, brown, green to yellow, pink, purple, orange, silver, bronze and gold.

Twill weaves are usually closely woven and are therefore stronger than plain weaves yet are more pliable and less prone to creasing. A very practical advantage is their ability to resist soiling and shed surface dirt. These qualities make is a very practical choice for combat wear – the indigo flak jacket, for instance, that is worn today by the charitable organisation, Handicap International, or the denim dungarees that were worn by the Royal Armoured Corps in WWII are just two examples out of many.

A twill is identified by the diagonal lines (also known as 'wales') that cross the surface; a diagram of the structure looks like a series of steps that can be varied in size according to the particular structure required – these are defined as 2/1, 3/2, etc. The first number represents the number of filling yarns that are crossed by the warp; the second number represents the number of filling yarns under which the warp passes. The angle of the lines can vary but most twill lines follow an angle of 45°; a 'steep' twill will follow an angle higher than this, whereas a 'reclining' twill will take a lower angle. In addition, the twill can run from left to right, or from right to left.

Denim is woven in yard-dyed cotton in a range of weights; most commonly, denim has a coloured warp and a white weft, whereas jean is piece-dyed and therefore will not develop the characteristic patterns of fading that contributes to denim's appeal. The weight of denim – which comes in a wide range, from 5 to 20 oz – will determine both the wearability and the look of a garment. For instance, a 20 oz denim is not going to bend and move for most garment uses & would therefore be suitable for a heavy duty furnishing or other use. On the other hand, a 5 oz denim is not going to be suitable for heavy denim jeans or jackets, but it would be ideal for any garment that requires a good draping quality or fine detail, such as shirts, skirts and dresses or children's clothing. The less the weight, the lighter, softer, and more loft (that is, the softness and fluffiness of the fibres) the denim will have. So although an 8oz denim is a little more pliable and soft than a 9 oz denim and the 9 oz sample is more pliable and softer than the 10 oz sample, they are all pretty much identical when it comes to their hardwearing qualities. The real difference lies in the drape and flexibility of the fabric. The standard weight for most denim jeans is 12 to 14 oz denim.

But denim can also be mixed with other fibres, such as linen, or wool (which is a reversion to its earlier history as a wool/linen or wool/cotton serge) or metallic fibres, such as Roberto Cavalli's indigo lurex. One example of this diversification is the Japanese Evisu jeans company, founded in 1991, who embellish denim with woven gold thread images or with hand-painting. Denim is a canvas – an ideal choice of sub-stratum for surface embroidery such as an elegant Louboutin high-heeled shoe, a potent symbol of exaggerated femininity that positions denim just about as far as it can be removed from its former masculine work-wear identity. It is clear that the levels of experimentation to which denim is receptive continue to evolve and through such innovation the future of denim will be secured.

The Denim Family; Fustian and Drabbet

"How can a man write poetically of serges and druggets?"
Dr Samuel Johnson (concerning the poem 'The Fleece' by Robert Dyer)

"For howsoever bad the devil can be in fustian or smock-frock (and he can be very bad in both), he is a more designing, callous, and intolerable devil when he sticks a pin in his shirt-front, and calls himself a gentleman..." Charles Dickens, 'Bleak House', 1852-3.

Before the First World War, work-wear was largely made up from a hard core of durable fabrics that were widely available and relatively cheap. They had evolved, undergoing many changes, through several centuries, and by the early 19th century Lancashire was the major manufacturing centre for competitively-priced cotton fabrics. In England, hemp, flax and woad (the last the source of blue dye before indigo became readily available and was later processed artificially) were common crops on peasant holdings, particularly in East Anglia, the West Country, Lancashire and Staffordshire. Linen, the product of indigenous flax, gradually became superceded by imported cotton which offered equally hardwearing but superior laundering qualities. A twilled linen/cotton or all cotton mix was commonly used for the farmer worker's smock – in England, this mix could be termed drabbet, drill, drilling, drugget, or jean, depending on the details of the weave structure, but similar materials were also available in other parts of Europe. In France, in particular, the blue worker's smock was a very familiar sight but it also featured prominently in England, and bears a striking resemblance to modern denim, particularly as it faded and revealed patterns of wear in much the same way as denim.

More recently, denim manufacturers (e.g., Isik Denim Tekstil, Istanbul) have revived a linen/cotton mix denim such as that featured in the high fashion mail-order catalogue, Toast, in 2006.

In the progression of cotton as the dominant fibre for work-wear, fustian is prominent as the oldest cotton fabric that is mentioned in English records, and is mentioned frequently in a wide range of records from the 16th to 19th centuries, both in England and in America. Fustian is one of the ancestors to modern denim, worn by men and women, and included herringbone weave, "pillows" (ticking) and 'lining jeans' as well as napped fabrics such as moleskin and ribbed fabrics such as corduroy, all of which were commonly worn for work-wear.

The countryman's smock, also known as a smock-frock, round-frock, or slop, was simply constructed from 2 rectangles or squares joined together, with openings for the arms and head, or with 4 additional rectangles/squares for the sleeves and collar. As this was the easiest way of constructing an upper body covering, it is hardly surprising that it was used universally throughout Europe. Evidence indicates that the smock had begun to be worn, as a practical protective layer, from the 17th century and it is likely that it had evolved from the generous sized overshirt that had been widely worn from the 16th century onwards.

In England, there were 3 styles of smock – the Reversible, the Coat-type, and the Shirt-type. The reversible was distinguished by two features: a small neck opening with main body sections identical, therefore there was no specific front or back; and the positioning of pockets that were set across, or vertically to, the side seams.

The Shirt smock featured a long front opening (but then was closed below that) and fastened part-way with several buttons; often these were metal buttons for extra strength. Lastly, the Coat smock had an opening that extended to the full length of the garment, with buttons all the way down to the hem. Despite these distinctions, there is no reliable evidence of a connection between the designs and the occupation of the wearer although there can be links with the locality in which they were made, particularly in relation to colour. Blue smocks, for instance, are associated with the Midlands, especially around Newark which was a centre of blue smock manufacturing; but the most common smocks were beige or fawn coarse twill or drabbet – Thomas Hardy referred to "Russian duck" (white) and "drabbet" (fawnish/brown) as the common materials of the smock-frock. Sometimes the material was coated with linseed oil, to waterproof it, but it did make the fabric rather sticky.

Smocks for special occasions were made of a superior quality white linen – these were the smocks for the Sunday service; most men would own at least 2 smocks, one for best and one for work. A common practice was to buy a plain smock and then smock and embellish it with embroidery.

By the second quarter of the 19th century, smocks were much admired and judged worthy as competition prizes in the 1838 Queen Victoria coronation celebrations. Two decades later, when the Rev. W.H.E. McKnight moved to Lydiard Manor, Gloucestershire, in 1852, he observed that the dress codes of his new neighbours were rather old-fashioned:

"At that time the villagers had not stepped out into the higher civilization of broadcloth. They still came to church in their snow-white smock-frocks which were here and there varied with a blue one, with its pattern in white thread conspicuous on the breast. On that morning there were a good many smock-frocks present..."

But it was precisely this quality – the attachment and respect for the past and its traditions and an indifference to the "higher civilization" of broadcloth - that appealed to members of the Arts & Crafts Movement that was just forming and had inspired William Morris, the leading light of the movement, to adopt the smock as a symbol of his commitment to socialist ideals and the revival of rural crafts.

Proudhon, like Morris, was an ardent socialist who also adopted the smock – and blue trousers – as a statement of his allegiance to the labouring classes. Here he is shown as the man of thought, rather than the man of physical toil.

An example of the short fustian smock suited for everyday wear. The white or pale colours of dairy smocks would reveal dirt and thus encourage the observance of hygienic standards required for dairy production. It has been claimed that blue denim hides dirt and thus contributes to its popularity as a work-wear material. Pyne, who produced 641 scenes of "national work" from 1802-1807, saw them of interest to: "the student of the picturesque". They were much admired and re-published; by

Ackermann in 1824, and by Dover in 1977, when they were ordered into 7 broad categories that co-incidentally correspond to the categories of use of denim.

Rural-worker's denim apron and country girl's drabbet smock. The apron was familiar within many male occupations – such as blacksmithing – but not in shepherds' dress. The girl's clothing, on the other hand, is more artistic licence than fact. Note the circular embroidery that emphasizes the contours of the girl's breasts – a feature intended to underscore the sexual meaning and moral message of this image that demonstrates the unreliability of some visual representations of rural dress. Only male rural-workers wore the embroidered smock, which would have been embroidered by their female relatives - most often, the wife – and the decoration, arranged in horizontal bands across the smock front, would in no way correspond with human anatomy, as it does here.

This is a particularly interesting example of the old fashioned smock caught on camera, probably the most significant inventions of this decade. The relationship of the artist's smock to the countryman's smock is an intimate one, and rooted in the increased romanticism of the artist as defender of 'true' cultural values, resulting in the polarization of art from industry. In reality, the smock was worn within many trades, such as butchers, fishmongers, tailors, and stonemasons, but it was the rural smock's appeal to the romantic imagination that steered the discriminating admirer towards it.

In this exercise in political propaganda and patriotism, the established sartorial code of the social strata of France is visually mapped. The farmer in the denim country-smock, donating money to the government with patriotic zeal, represents the rural community, whilst the dress of the male figure on the far right represents the urban sector.

Smocks, especially those intended for special occasions only, were made to order from women who worked at home, but smocks for everyday work-wear were increasingly manufactured in small factories, often in areas were flax was or had been grown. Haverhill in Suffolk is an example of a small rural town that rapidly expanded over 40 years in the 19th century due to the increased demand for these goods; drabbet, the fabric commonly used for smocks, was produced on steam-powered looms and turned into ready-made smocks by Gurteen's, whose success represented "a major leap forward in the business from just supplying drabbet, fustian and cotton cloths to other businesses". The smock was worn by the respectable with pride, but it was also coveted by the disreputable who often resorted to theft in order to acquire one, and it could also represent the badge of servitude. The Stamford Mercury, 20th May, 1836, published the description of an absconder from a 'House of Industry' for paupers who was wearing: "a long smock and fustian frock, and a pair of moderate cord small-clothes"; and at a Hertfordshire trial held in 1845, the defendant, a notorious 17 year old thief recently discharged from the County prison, was charged with stealing a labourer's smock frock valued at 1s. Other trial reports indicate that the smock was worn as a disguise by gangs of wayside robbers in order to fake respectability.

By the end of the 19th century, the smock had almost entirely disappeared. Whilst it had not been widely worn, it had become emblematic of a romantic, bucolic idyll, endorsed by aesthetes such as John Ruskin, and prolonged by Ackermann's publication of Pyne's work in 1824 that extended the romanticism of rural life against the backdrop of increased industrialism. However, The Royal Commission Report on agricultural labour, undertaken from 1893-1894, concluded that: "The old smock-frock is very nearly extinct" and further commented that rural labourers dressed like the "class above them" (Rachel Worth, *The Englishness of English Dress*). Furthermore, the 'peasant' smock had become anachronistic and dangerous in the increasingly mechanized farming and industrial world. For the Arts & Crafts romantics, it was symbolic of anti-modernity. Ironically, this sentimentalism preserved it in other forms and contexts, such as infants' and children's dress with smocked bodices, made very fashionable by Liberty's of London, that continues to be a very popular choice for those who prefer the image of innocence for their offspring. For Thomas Hardy, the rustic smock signified the lamentable loss of the old order that had given way to the new order of urban sophistication: "You shall change this smock-frock for a real cloth jacket, and your thick boots for polished shoes." (*A Changed Man*, 1913).

The countryman's smock was part of folk fiction of English rural life, "invested with ideals about the supposed stability of English country-life", and had equal resonance within French political ideology. This was the reason why it was adopted by those who polarised the rural from the industrial, whilst they enjoyed a lifestyle was far removed from the harsh realities of living off the land.

The Apron – The alternative to smock

A variation on the countryman's drugget smock, denim also has a place in the history of work-wear aprons that were worn by women and men labouring on the land. One example is the full-length denim apron worn by immigrant Japanese women who worked on the sugar cane plantations on Tahiti from the later 19th century; the strength of denim protected them from the sharp stalks of the canes. The English version of the manual worker's denim apron – a common protective garment worn in many male occupations, such as blacksmithing – is clearly depicted in Holman Hunt's painting 'The Hireling Shepherd' (1851). Then, as now, blue denim was particularly popular; today a similar, androgynous, blue denim apron is available from Muji, the world-wide Japanese store.

Denim and its association with military and naval uniforms

The prominence of military uniforms in the 19th century is a significant stimulus to the expansion of the denim family. The frequency of military conflict in Europe raised the profile of military clothing to such a pitch that the fashion for dressing small children in pint-sized versions became a widespread gesture to patriotism. In Britain, still proudly protective of its naval supremacy, this fashion took the form of the sailor suit that was endorsed by Queen Victoria who dressed the heir to the throne in a white linen suit (a duck jumper) that is now preserved in The National Maritime Museum at Greenwich. Similar suits were equally popular in other countries, including France and Sweden. This was not a fashion that was restricted to boy's wear, as a girl's version of the woollen serge sailor suit had developed by the last quarter of the 19th century, and was widely worn, as seen in the photograph of Lillian Myers, taken some time between 1883 and 1887 by a London photographer. Curiously, early versions of ladies' cricketing dress and boating dress also borrowed features – usually the sailor collar – as a sign of outdoor physical activity.

Anne Buck viewed children's dress as the "testing ground for adult change, for the entry of new garments into the main stream of fashion" (*Clothes and the Child*) and noted that it was strongly influenced by work-wear. Popular trends in children's wear, such as the nautical style or dungarees, centre around two factors: firstly, an idealisation of childhood reinforced by pedagogical theories of 'free expression' in play and, secondly, increased structured leisure activities for children. Denim thus satisfies the demand for comfort and practicality in children's dress from both pragmatic and ideological perspectives. Possibly the earliest surviving examples of denim as a clothing material for children's wear are preserved in the Wisconsin Historical Society collection; these are simple garments that have seen much rough and tumble, and have been patched and repaired to extend their life. In June, 1921 one Gertrude Killfeather registered with the US Patent Office a dress in the style of a sailor's tunic with a sailor collar that "may be made up of denim, or other durable material..."

Today, diverse yet co-existing examples of children's dress such as Junior Gaultier, nautically-inspired, white denim jeans for boys; Arts & Crafts, rural-influenced, smocked dresses from Liberty's; and Levi's Red Label mini work-wear overalls for infants, map the significant distance that denim has travelled from adult work-wear in the 19th century to high fashion in the 21st century child's wardrobe. Many schools in the UK specifically ban denim and corduroy – those familiar work-wear fabrics – from school uniforms that are not otherwise subjected to rigid regulations.

Military and Naval uniforms

The prevalence of denim in military clothing had become so pervasive by the mid 20th century that it featured in popular terminology. Beale's Dictionary of Slang states that the Durham Light Infantry fighting in Tunisia in 1943 was known as: 'The Denim Light Infantry'. Newly introduced uniforms were often made of denim as an economic expedient, such as the first British Home Guard Air Raid Precautions uniforms that consisted of overalls made from 'Bluette No.T.500', a denim fabric that repelled dirt and oil. Female air raid wardens were issued with their own uniforms also made from Bluette, whilst the ARP nurse's uniform was made of a lighter-weight denim material. Later the denim ARP overalls were replaced by wool serge when the style of the uniform was developed to a more formal style. The Danish army, however, replaced their woollen uniforms with denim – as evidence of Danish modernity perhaps? The British Land Army uniforms of the First and Second World Wars also utilized denim, particularly for the farm-worker's and dairy maid's smocks. which were made from white denim. And in the USA, denim uniform spilt over into civvy street in 1925 when a stockbroking company issued a blue denim smock to all staff in order to: "give an air of neatness to the offices which cannot be attained, save through uniform dress".

Popular cultural associations between naval and military wear and denim would suggest that denim has a long-established relationship with combat gear. On the contrary, although it is strongly linked, the degree to which it was used is comparatively small compared to denim's antecedents, such as serge. As denim and jean were often interchangeable terms, and the only difference between them was the piece-dyed jean versus the coloured warp/white weft structure of denim, and the relative weights of the two fabrics, it is appropriate to regard them as inter-related variations on a theme of practicality. Denim/jean was most commonly used for the collar in naval uniforms – as seen in Rozanne Hawksley's tribute to her grand-mother, Alice Hunter, who supported her children by working as a seamstress for the Admiralty. The reverse of the sailor collar was backed with a blue/white or grey/white striped jean material; whereas the navy blue knitted Royal Navy tunic sported blue denim epaulettes. In the summer, the uniforms that were such a familiar sight in the English naval dockyards in the 1950's and '60's were made of white drill – that is, the same fibre and structure as denim, but of solid colour. Despite the links with the discipline of the forces, denim in the 1970's began to represent the release from inhibition and seemingly pointless rules; and, as the textile review Ciba, stated in the Jan/Feb issue: "world demand continues unabated for denim jeans in all colours, but especially blue" (1974). The Daily Mirror fashion correspondent Liz Smith confessed the following month: "As blue denim addicts, we can't, it seems, get enough of the stuff". The popular attraction to denim appeared to be boundless.

It is clear that military uniforms in high street surplus stores in the 1960's (a form of recycling) raised public awareness of the denim family and most certainly contributed to the rise of denim as a fashionable fabric, not least because those teenagers who first began to scour the army surplus outlets could be guaranteed to feel and look like urban rebels. The position of young people in society was changing, the period of youthfulness was extending, and their taste was consequently more influential and capable of leading adult fashion. Wearing denim, particularly embellished with camouflage patterns, was a counter-uniform to uniform, signaling a contempt and lack of respect for the two world wars that were fought in and endured by their parents and grandparents. It was hardly surprising that the growing vogue for denim aroused both disapproval and anxiety within a broad sector of the population. .

However, there is one section where denim camouflage dress continues to be accepted and regularly worn by the non-military and that is within rural working life. Contemporary gamekeepers, who no longer walk anywhere and don't have to worry about keeping warm, have replaced the traditional corduroys and tweeds with camouflage drill that offers concealment but little protection from the elements.

Thus, the cultural phenomenon of denim in the second half of the 20th century is a process by which it becomes symbolic of playtime/ leisuretime and urban culture, and paradoxically discards and preserves its work-wear associations. Denim has persistently retained a spurious romantic association with the nobility of hard labour and the adventurous pioneer, linked to the romantic myth of rural culture as an escape from the over-regulation of urban life. Yet, there seems to be no limit to the work-wear potential for denim to be enlisted - in the USA 13.5 oz denim jeans with a "unique 5.11 twist" are advertised as: 'Great for Probation Officers'! It seems that their particular selling feature for the arm of the law, the facility of a "concealed carry" for items such as 'backup' and 'standard handcuffs' , might equally appeal to the offender!

Denim in Art/Craft Textiles

Recycling is a recurrent theme in the life of denim. Until denim became high fashion, it was a cheap fabric that could sustain repeated repairs, such as that seen in the patched jeans in Woodville's painting 'War News from Mexico' (1848). For the black families living in the area of Gee's Bend, Alabama, necessity led to the development of a remarkable culture of sewing, in a free-form style, of quilts made from recycled denim work clothes. These quilts came to light in the 1960's, when the growing movement for Black American suffrage was spear-headed by Martin Luther King. As a result the quilts acquired significant cultural status as emblems of self-sufficiency and innate creativity. The use of old work clothes went beyond the frugality of recycling and became commemorative of the family wearers and the wider community history. A family photograph belonging to one of the quilt maker's shows numerous children wearing worn denim dungarees, like their father's, who stands in the foreground. The Gee's Bend quilts now command considerable attention and admiration – they have evolved over the decades, are made of brighter colours and different fabrics, but the original examples with their fragile denim remains still project an extraordinary combination of pathos and power. Rozanne Hawksley's installation work similarly invites us to peer into another world, as culturally remote from us as Alabama, USA. Themes of war, death and loss against a background of religious belief are prominent, but a sense of continuity through emotional connections is also discernible, and her work – like those of the quilt-makers – is both a homage to the past and a material embodiment of the experience of hardship and grief through the ritual of sewing.

Recycling was a topic that regularly appeared in a new publication, The Golden Hands Encyclopaedia of Craft, that was successfully launched in the 1970's. The instruction to readers to cut up their jeans and turn them into lampshades struck the chord of self-sufficiency principles that laid the foundations of an alternative, anti-materialist lifestyle philosophy in which denim became emblematic of egalitarian principles.

ON WEARING DENIM

"Don't 'iron' them, they're just there, and there's no alteration between work and play."

> "I always wear jeans to dress down; they have a weekend feel to me, I would never wear them to a meeting or for going out to dinner in a posh restaurant. I would never wear them in my twenties and thirties as I saw them as common and I wanted to be different. I only bought a pair once I got into my fourties and I felt quite liberated. The cut or shape of jeans can make me feel different as well, depending on if they are ripped, loose and faded (young and trendy) or hideous high waisted and tight ones (an old has-been) and as for straight legged drain pipe tight ones, well I shudder at the thought, lets not even go there!!!"

"Wet denim does not feel good: but everyone has taken the risk of going out in jeans knowing it might but hoping it won't rain and then it does and you stay with wet strides for the rest of the day."

> "I think you have to be very careful about wearing jeans and a denim jacket - the denim suit look is a high-risk fashion strategy unless you are Kris Kristofferson or Dolly Parton."

"'Dad's jeans' can also be highly suspect. These garments are often of an anonymous brand, are shapeless but sport a killer crease down the front. Sometimes "Dad's jeans" are made of a material that could be described as denim-esque or like denim."

"Clearly any jean with an elasticated waistband is just wrong, unless you are aged three or under, when it is acceptable."

"I think denim dungarees are an effective way of appearing like a lumbering buffoon."

"Stretch denim and that marble effect is so wrong."

"I wouldn't wear denim to work and I don't think you should, unless you are a cowboy or rock star."

"I always feel at home in denim as opposed to other fabrics. I guess I'm unconcerned what folk think."

"I love the colour and the softness of the fabric when it's worn in."

"Denim shapes itself to your body so it fits really well and is comfortable. You feel you look good and feel more confident."

"I enjoy wearing it because the material itself doesn't go out of fashion, only the style. However, I wouldn't dream of wearing it to a smart event. I didn't wear any denim at all for about five years, partly because I was a student but didn't want to look like one."

"It's a fabric that's great for everyone, from tots (if it's soft enough) to grandads - and I should know, I live with the latter and he looks great in jeans! I hate the grubby over-dye look of some fashion jeans, it makes me want to give them a good wash."

"It has a nice, casual look and feel but these days I like dressing up jeans with nice tops, shoes and jewellery. I wouldn't feel right going anywhere really "posh" in them, though I know people do. Denim is super comfortable - I have everything from a skirt to a shirt in it, but in different textures (some stretchy)."

"The fabric is often too cold, stiff, or heavy. I don't like all-blue clothing, and there's always those unnecessary rivets and/or blouson jacket side-strap things which look naff, and stitching all over the place where it's not needed. Leave it on the hanger. Walk away now. Do not wear."

"Only have 2 items (which I really like) but on the whole denim doesn't suit me. So in terms of feeling different it would be 'feeling wrong'."

"By the 1970s jeans were ubiquitous and worn by (say) students, everyday for everything."

"Optima are a design agency BUT unlike many others I don't let my designers wear jeans. I associate jeans with manual labour or a student casual look, not business.

So, jeans are for going out and the weekend and DIY jobs because my old jeans still wear well."

"You could say I feel 'free', relaxed and back to basics in my Jeans."

"It takes forever to dry."

"It improves with age."

"I love the colour and the softness of the fabric when it's worn in.'

"Biggest denim crime – stonewashed jeans."

"Denim is the most widely used and popular clothing because it speaks, tells it's tale, provides a narrative, implies a history, imparts meaning, bears the tracks and traces, stains and memories of its passage; it is a marker of time."

"As Kato-san says 'However, whilst man is a tool for completing a garment, the garment cannot be complete without the personality of the wearer.'"

DENIM IN CONTEMPORARY FASHION

Denim, the relatively cheap to produce fabric that has both durability and glamour, has, over the decades, become an important influence in our society.

No longer thought of as just a hardwearing material for industry, it is now regarded as a blank canvas to be embellished by fashion designers. Street and Couture fashion are crossing boundaries, using this simplistic fabric in the most innovative of styles and decoration.

What is the interest in this most basic of fabrics? It is cold in the winter, conversely hot in summer and when wet it takes ages to dry. It fades when over washed, takes years to wear out and is stiff and hard on the skin. In the last decade this perception of the most universally known cloth has changed dramatically as industry uses technology to manufacture the "must have" denim, experimenting with weights, dyes and surfaces. Fashion designers are becoming innovative with pattern cutting and surface decoration in an attempt to revitalise and instil glamour into an everyday basic material.

Jeans are by far the most common fashion garment produced from denim. However, lately it has appeared in the guise of dresses, coats and accessories on the runways of the most traditional Couture houses of Europe such as Dior, Chanel and Christian Lacroix.

The American film industry established the traditional denim garment as the trade mark, or badge of office, for the misfit or rebel. Marlon Brando and James Dean were perhaps the most influential of this new breed of screen actors. The traditional jean became a symbol of subversive behaviour and was quickly adopted by sections of society who were nonconformist in their lifestyle or political beliefs. It became a uniform for human tribes easily recognisable by their code of dress. Before the 60's and 70's all that was available in the denim fashion stakes were jeans, blouson jackets and the dungaree or 'bib' ensemble, all based on the American West workwear, with traditional rivets, pockets and styling. The only concession to styling was the replacement of copper rivets with a cross formation in stitch to strengthen the easily torn areas of the garment such as the pockets, and this was only changed on certain brands at the request of cowboys who were concerned that the metal damaged their saddles. Images of miners digging for gold and cowboys herding cattle are evoked with the brand names of Levi and Lee Cooper. Changes were small and concerned only with detail as previously mentioned and were usually for practical or economic reasons. No changes were made for fashion purposes or individuality.

Elio Fiorucci, credited with inventing the concept of designer denim, defined the disco era of the 70's and 80's with the labels skintight Buffalo '70 jeans. Eminent New Yorkers such as Jacqueline Kennedy Onassis and Bianca Jagger were all devotees of this new approach to the most mundane of materials. The Italians made jeans sexy and desirable, but, most importantly, they realised the potential in cutting jeans to fit the female form, rather than women buying men's jeans and spending endless hours in a cold bath for the sole purpose of shrinking them to fit.

The 60's saw the emergence of free love, drug culture and experimental music. These three combined elements brought the emergence of individually customised jeans and jackets. Flower Power and anti-war symbols, hand crafted in embroidery and print suddenly appeared on denim. A form of decoration, not only powerful in it's political message, but creative, individual and un-commercial. Insertions of floral patterned fabric were sewn into the legs from the knee down to create bellbottoms and flares. These denim jeans, originally massed produced, became unique with added flamboyant personal embellishment - often crudely executed, and craft based.

Today's decoration, mostly manufactured by new technology, is decidedly more considered regarding the placing of the design on the finished garment.

In the last decade, conceptual fashion designers Martin Margiela and Hussein Chalayan have both used denim in their collections. The former, in his Stockman collection for Autumn/Winter 2000-2001, included a pair of destroyed denim oversized jeans and jacket 200% larger than the average body size. Worn on the runway by a 'size zero' model, the look was dramatic as well as intellectually modern. British designer Hussein used computer imagery in his Echoform memory dress collection for Autumn/ Winter 1999-2000. This computer animation consisted of a series of near-identical denim dresses that had pockets and stitching added and taken away to represent memory and loss. Each dress bore traces of the previous garment.

Yohi Yamamoto, drawing on his interests in antique western tailoring and contemporary Japan, produced a jacket and skirt based on the American Levi jacket and jean from the end of the last century. The jacket was a very subtle interpretation of the traditional denim blouson with the addition of a lighter weight black jersey jacket attached as a lining. The skirt was again a mixture of black jersey and denim. Voluminous in shape, the skirt was cut to resemble half a jean opened up on one side with the jersey skirt forming the rest of the design. In recent years Junya Watanaba has produced a denim collection which resembled an Edwardian costume with a twist. The skirts, fishtailed and extremely tight, teamed with a jacket in twill denim that was ruched down the front by the clever placing of buttons, distorting the cloth.

For other fashion designers, particularly the European fashion houses, concerns with structure have been replaced: they have embellished and decorated, rather than experiment with concept and innovation of form. The Italians are perhaps the frontrunners in this direction. Their cultural love of pattern and surface decoration over the centuries has produced some interesting additions to the denim culture. In 2002, Roberto Cavalli produced an embroidered trouser suit on light blue cotton denim. The images of interlocking flowers evoked memories of the hand embroidered waistcoats of the 17th Century but, of course, these flowers were machine manufactured with the advance of new technology. In recent years he produced, for his defusion range 'Just Cavalli', a Hussar jacket heavily embroidered with gold thread and trimmed down the front and cuffs with fox fur. This was pure glamour, with an historical reference to the more Romantic approach to dress of the Napoleonic Wars. The same collection saw skin tight jeans encrusted with beads and jewels. Denim had become desirable and sumptuous overnight. Once a classless material it has, through embellishment, become expensive with the use of traditional textile skills such as beading and embroidery. Techniques that are labour intensive and usually reserved for evening wear or embroidered on silk, are now directed towards the most basic of materials. The embroidery is not always necessarily machined, but is sometimes hand crafted in the Far East. How was this approach different from the customized jackets and jeans of the 1970's? The answer is not only in the quality of the embroidery, machine or hand produced, but in the applied design which is usually lavish and intricate. Sophistication replaced the ethnic ethos of the 70's.

As a result, these garments were worn during the day as works of art, to be admired and coveted. Suddenly, it became acceptable to visit a fashionable restaurant or appear on the red carpet in denim, as long as it was expensive and above all a designer label. An individual's bank balance could be instantly assessed by the make of denim they wore.

Jeans were teamed with Chanel jackets and other Couture accessories. All very acceptable to those who ran exclusive establishments with celebrity status!

Traditional printed and embroidered surface decoration is only one aspect of embellishment. Fashion designers all over the world were, and still are, keen to design clothing made with denim but with their own signature style. Vivienne Westwood picked up the gauntlet in 1991 with her 'Cut and Slash' for both men and women. Historical textile reference was the inspiration behind this collection. The cutting technique of the 16th century, which entailed a sharp shaped instrument being hammered into the cloth in a pattern formation, leaving a frayed edge around the cut shape, was applied to denim cloth very successfully. The white warp yarn of the denim material emphasized the cut frayed edge against the Indigo weft yarn, producing a dramatic slashed effect.

'Deconstruction' - the destruction of a cloth and its reconstruction into an entirely different look - is not a new concept, but it is one that has produced some interesting effects with denim. Distressed denim originated from everyday wear and tear, producing a well worn pair of jeans, softer in texture with a few threadbare patches, usually on the knees and back pockets and a colour tone that was patchy due to constant washing. It then became fashionable to wear a pair of distressed denims, but, as the effect could not be created instantly, industry obliged by distressing denim by mechanical means. Worn by A-list 'celebs' such as David Beckham, they became an instant success. British fashion designer Alexander McQueen presented a long denim skirt frayed in small squares and reassembled for Givenchy Haute Couture in 1998, while Dolce and Gabbana for Spring/ Summer 2001 produced both horizontally and vertically slashed denim jeans held together by safety pins, reminiscent of the British Punk street fashion era. In 2002, Junya Watanabe paid homage to the peasant-hippie 70's revival and swept Milan fashion week with his collection of denim 'rags'. Denim was faded, ripped and torn by hand, patchworked, and then ingeniously constructed into jackets, skirts and jeans in a contemporary version of the hippie prairie look. This effect has since reappeared in Christopher Kane's Spring/Summer London collection 2008, as ripped bodices and jeans in light blue denim. No doubt it will continue to seen on the runway in years to come not only in street fashion, but also as Couture.

New technology has, in recent years, produced a fascinating array of techniques which have been applied to denim. Experimentation with laser has come into its own, particularly with the requirement of an image on the cloth that has not been printed. Lasers are making giant strides into the lighter manufacturing industries, including the fashion and apparel industries. Denim engraving is a new, fast growing technical process. It is used as a bleaching and cutting tool, creating intricate patterns and designs on uncut denim and on the finished garment. Traditional distressing techniques such as acid washing, sandblasting, whisker washing and 'slub' weaving have been replaced by a method that provides detail and sophistication. Lasers can reproduce photographic imagery, fake 3D effects such as embossing, embroidering and apparent tears and mends. Before this new laser technology, sanding, ripping and other distressing effects were done by hand, as in the Couture collections. Consequently, no two garments would be exactly the same. The finished effect was time consuming and would be personalised by the operator, thus providing an extremely labour intensive garment. Labour, in human resources, costs money whilst quantity reduces cost. Laser manufactured fashion denims with an image created by a CAD pattern process can retail at well over 100 pounds sterling. Stone washed effects, which once required monitoring of stones in washing machines to attain certain degrees of distressing, are now produced more quickly, by comparison. This may well keep costs down, but all garments have an identical look while still commanding Couture prices.

Europa, the Prato based Italian fabric manufactures, who supply to designers of both Street Fashion and Couture, have produced an innovative approach to denim. Surface decoration consists of machine embroidery, jacquard weaving and print techniques. Designs are flamboyant and sourced from traditional European patterns, but the combination of techniques used are innovative and contemporary. Europa recently produced a denim fabric that had been flocked, overprinted with gold and then washed. The end result was a raised velvet like surface with particles of gold embedded in the flocking, giving an antique quality. They also manufacture jacquard weaves that have Couture logos in repeat pattern. The celebrated Louis Vuitton monogrammed denim handbag designed by Marc Jacobs in 2005 brought a look that was chic and casual to an expensive accessory. In 2006, Issey Miyake presented a collection of men's jeans that had a 'splash' design translated by woven technology.

These Italian manufacturers are not only concerned with decorative surfaces but also the yarn composition of the fabric itself.

In New York in 2007, Diesel showed jeans and jumpsuits with copper laminated finishes. Stretch denim coated with gold was moulded to the skin while micro-shorts were woven in denim, mixed with lurex and lame yarns. Fine steel had been woven with traditional denim to create a shimmering, pliant fabric for smock tops, full-skirted shirtwaist dresses and short ra-ra skirts. Brands like Diesel are part of a surge of small denim-based cult companies like True Religion, Seven for all Mankind, Rock and Republic and Paper Denim & Cloth, to name just a few. According to the fashion industries trade magazine Women's Wear Daily (WWD) there are said to be over 700 denim-based brands in existence to date, all competing with new technology, decoration and cut. 2008 has seen the demise of the skinny jean in favour of the wide legged, high waisted denim trouser. Fashion is influencing choice as many dare not be seen in a pair of jeans that are not deemed 'cool.' So we throw away last years style and lust over the newest design in the glossy magazines, thinking that we will look like the 'size zero' supermodel portrayed if we buy the product advertised. Alexandra Shulman, Editor of British Vogue, commented that denim is back for 2008, with Karl Lagerfeld for Chanel designing shorts, jackets and bikinis for his Spring collection. However, she expresses surprise that even young students are prepared to pay over £100 for a pair of jeans. Gone are the days when owning a pair of 501's was enough to fulfil your denim wardrobe. Today there are numerous choices in the brand, the cut, the application and the composition of the material and colour. Denim does not have to be traditional indigo, for example in the late 90's black was the colour to be seen wearing, now it can vary from tones of black and blue to just plain white. Denim has held its ground over the decades and is now so big in all aspects of the fashion market that Premier Vision in Paris has dedicated a whole trade fair to the fabric and its application.

Environmentalists have contributed to the production of denim, particularly at the turn of the 21st century. In 1989, Katharine Hamnett discovered that conventional cotton agriculture was responsible for 10,000 deaths per annum from accidental pesticide poisoning. She decided to change the industry from within and launched her "Clean Up or Die" collection. In 1995 Hamnett returned from showing in Paris to launch her eco friendly denim collection, but her passion for environmental and ethical values was not taken seriously by the industry until the recent awareness of global warming. Hamnett was ahead of her time. Since then huge steps have been taken to manufacture the most organically-leaning and ecologically-savvy denim. This applies notably to the production of the material itself, but also to the treatment of the work force involved. This way of thinking has been taken up by designer Sharkah Chakra. Her organic jeans use "the Free Trade talents of indigenous indigo farmers, dyeing masters and tailors". The company's philosophy is "to make the world's best and only hand made denim using a simple age old concept of treating others as you wish to be treated". Fashion with a conscience is here to stay and does not mean shapeless earth toned garments. It will become more expensive to retail as more human resources are required in the manufacture. While the West struggles with its conscience regarding Fair Trade manufacturing of denim, the Far East is experimenting with chemistry. In 2003, a Japanese designer produced jeans impregnated with sarginine, an amino acid said to keep the skin youthful. Fatty acids in the fabric used to make jeans, developed by Teijin Wow, also moisturised, smelt fragrant and fought bacteria. Some jeans even claimed to help reduce cellulite through impregnated chemicals.

"Imitation is the sincerest form of flattery." So powerful has the influence of denim become that it has been used as a faux or, in some cases, a homage with various manufacturers and designers. Jakob Schlaepfer, the Swiss embroidery company who produces fabrics for the Couture houses has recently manufactured printed sequins to look like denim as lengths of fashion fabric. Issey Miyake's Pleats Please range produced a skirt that was printed like a traditional denim straight skirt but pleated, whilst French fashion designer Jean-Charles De Castelbajac presented a dress printed with the stitch outlines of a pair of jeans. Even a pair of leather trousers printed to look like denim has been spied in store at Printemps Paris.

How will denim evolve during the rest of the century? Will it be applied to other areas besides fashion and be seen in the domestic interior? In the 60's and 70's it was used in interior design but has not yet returned as the must have product in the home or office. Where fashion leads, interior design usually follows. The next few years will be interesting as technology, social and political issues are reflected in the most versatile of materials. Social and political bodies are increasingly using denim to promote personal wellbeing for women and children. 'Wear your jeans to work days' are used by American manufacturers Lee to support breast cancer awareness along side the cult brand J & Company who specifically produced a collection with the Pink Ribbon emblem embroidered in Swarovski crystals. Here in the UK, Jeans for Genes have used the same concept to draw attention to research into genetic disorders in children.

Denim has proved over the decades to be the blank canvas of our age, measuring society and its thinking.

© Val Beattie 2008

WORDS PEOPLE ASSOCIATE
WITH THE WORD DENIM

Vision. Touch. Blue. Movement. Define. Buttons. Rebel. Rock'n'roll. Freedom. Daring. Sunglasses. Leather. Punks. Jeans. Jacket.

Or ten words would be:

"For the man who doesn't have to try, too hard."

Blue. Black. Soft. Clean. Comfortable. Sexy. Hardwearing. Rugged. Outdoors. American. Standard. Bleached. Worn. Cotton. Aftershave. Casual. DIY. Hardwork. Stonewash. Levis. Quo. Indigo. Overproduced. Chav. Uncomfortable. Cowboys. Sassy. Weekend. Americana. blue selvedge loom 32 levis jeans. Indigo velvet doughnut rivet baby. blue gene baby. Bluesfallingdownlikerain. Love. Lee Cooper. Skiffle. Creative. Personal. Obsessive. Detailed. Shibui. Inventive. Humourous. Playful.

SOME 'FACTS' ABOUT DENIM

Summarised by Phil Cosker, from Cotton Inc USA © data

Through brand, price, and spreading worldwide popularity, denim has become one of the most recognized fabrics in the apparel industry. Consumers in many countries, such as the United States and Germany, have worn and loved denim jeans for years, while others are just beginning to appreciate denim's comfort and style and to incorporate it into their wardrobes. As new denim markets have emerged and jeans ownership has reached an all-time high, global consumers' love of denim, denim purchase patterns, and love of cotton all have increased, according to the latest Global Lifestyle Monitor, a global consumer attitude study conducted by Cotton Council International and Cotton Incorporated.

Denim continues to be one of the most popular items in global consumers' wardrobes. The percentage of global consumers who agreed that "my wardrobe is full of denim and I love wearing it" or "I enjoy wearing denim regularly" rose to an all-time high of 64% in 2006. Affinity for denim was highest among German consumers (87%), followed by consumers in the United States (78%) and Colombia (76%). Since the inception of the Global Lifestyle Monitor in 1999, love of denim has grown most in the European countries of Germany (by 33 percentage points), the United Kingdom (22 points), and Italy (17 points). Denim's increasing popularity is also reflected in the percentage of consumers who plan to purchase denim in the future. Nearly two-thirds of global consumers (outside of the United States) said that they planned to purchase as much or more denim in the next 12 months as in the past year.

Denim Ownership Is On the Rise

Around the world, consumers' closets are full of denim jeans, shirts, skirts, dresses, shorts, and jackets and consumers are continuing to expand their denim wardrobes. The average number of denim garments owned per global consumer increased from 11 in 1999 to 13 in 2006, with the most growth in jeans and skirts. Consumers reported owning the most denim garments in the United States (16), Thailand (16), and Colombia (15) and the fewest in China (4) and India (2). Nonetheless, almost every consumer owns denim—in 2006, 94% of global consumers owned at least one denim garment, up 4 percentage points since 2003.

The denim item most commonly owned by global consumers is jeans, with an average ownership of 7 pairs up 29% since 1999. Nearly nine out of ten global consumers own at least one pair of denim jeans, and they wear them an average of three days a week. Jeans remain most popular among Americans, who own an average of 9 pairs, followed by consumers in Colombia (8 pairs), the United Kingdom (8 pairs), and Germany (7 pairs). German consumers showed the largest increase in denim jeans ownership, which was up an average of 2 pairs since 2003. Brazilian, Japanese, Chinese, and Indian consumers were below the global average for jeans ownership. However, although Indian consumers owned the fewest pairs of denim jeans, they had the second largest growth rate in jeans ownership, indicating that India may be an emerging denim market to watch.

Denim garments owned per global consumer:

7 pairs of jeans
2 pairs of shorts
2 shirts
2 skirts*
1 jacket
1 dress*

*Female consumers only.

Expenditures on Denim Jeans

Denim jeans continued to claim a significant part of Global Monitor consumers' clothing budgets: 6% to 14% of total apparel expenditures. Over the last year, global consumers spent an average of $921 on apparel, including $99 (11%) on denim jeans. As a percentage of total apparel expenditures, jeans had the largest share among consumers in Colombia (14%), Germany (13%), and Italy (13%). Italian consumers spent the most on apparel ($1,716) and likewise the most on denim jeans ($217). Indian consumers spent the least on apparel ($190) and the smallest share of their apparel budget on denim jeans ($12, or 6%). Instead of jeans, Indian consumers preferred to spend on dresses, saris, and Punjabi suits, which accounted for over half (54%) of their apparel purchases.

MOVIES PEOPLE ASSOCIATED WITH DENIM

Girl on a Motorcycle (wasn't that leather?). Possibly the worst movie of all time. *Giant. Cool Hand Luke. Woodstock.* Old cowboy films such as *Calamity Jane. The Graduate. On the Waterfront. Badlands* (Malick'73) : Sheen as Kit as Dean as Starkweather ...Sissy. Spacek as Holly...specifically the *Love is Strange* sequence. *Merry Go Round* (Rivette'78/'83..) ... Little Joe D'Allasandro and Maria Schneider ... the indigo set against the green of the golf course and the colours of the beach. *Key Largo* (Huston'48). *One Flew Over the Cuckoo's Nest.* The group that Jonny Rocco leaves shut out in the hurricane. Rodd Redwing and Jay Silverheels, (what jeans are they wearing? I need to look at the clip). *Jailhouse Rock. Suddenly One Summer. Peyton Place. Summer Holday.*

CUT OFF IN MY PRIME

As a teenager, my taste in music, my circle of friends, the places we went and the associated cultural expectations dictated the wearing of denim. In particular, they dictated the wearing of a denim jacket. I had a few over the years, but they were all the same – Levi's Red Tab. As far as I was concerned, no other jacket had the same kudos, the same cachet of cool. The small red, or sometimes orange label was a stroke of marketing genius. Nothing overtly shouting its identity, yet noticeable at a distance; saving one from the ignominy of wearing a lesser brand or, god forsake, no brand at all.

To be at its best, the jacket needed to be tight fitting, the sleeves slightly pulled up, and the denim needed to show the faded, worn look of constant use, even eventually worn through at collar and cuffs. Yet the status of Levi Strauss & Co. was such that even wearing a brand new, dark blue jacket was deemed socially acceptable. Pin badges were worn on the front, but the back of the jacket was the canvas on which to paint one's personality – and people did paint, and patch, and even cover them with bar towels. Three themes were considered acceptable – rock music, motorcycles and alcohol. Personally, I didn't go much for patches of bands, but preferred to colourfully embroider their names directly into the denim in an arc across the shoulders or in a line across the bottom of the back of the jacket. This was clearly an act of inclusion and exclusion, drawing a ring around those I related to and simultaneously putting up a fence between those with different tastes in music and myself. Care had to be taken in the choice of bands committed to this canvas – authenticity was all – you are what you listen to.

When I started to ride a motorcycle and go to rallies (which involved lengthy camping weekends and copious amounts of alcohol) the denim jacket took on a whole new form. Leather jackets had to be worn – for safety, for warmth, but mainly for self-identity – so the denim jacket became a 'cut-off'. The sleeves were torn from the jacket, leaving strands of material dangling (one work colleague of mine failed to understand this distinction and embarrassed himself by having his mother cut the sleeves neatly off and hem them! How we laughed). The jacket was then worn over the leather in the manner of a waistcoat.

Again, the back portrayed one's affiliations – this time to a marque of bike, embroidered or sewn-on patches. Rallying involved the collection of the metal enamelled badges provided as proof of attendance. These were fastened securely to the cut-off, the number of badges a status symbol of one's involvement with the scene. Heavily badged cut-offs could look (and weigh) like chain mail. A life in heavy metal. A friend of mine had so many on a well-worn cut-off that the whole thing gave way during a blast down the motorway and was lost forever, despite lengthy attempts to backtrack and locate it.

Inevitably, being covered in metal badges, the cut-off was never washed. Exposed to the elements, dirt accumulated, along with sweat and spilt beer. Engine oil became ingrained in the cloth after roadside repairs. My own had other embellishments – a clip onto which was attached my pewter tankard (standard fare – safer than carrying glasses around everywhere and easier to hold onto when drunk or dancing!) and a memento from my first motorbike: my first sparkplug, threaded through one of the buttonholes. I wore my cut-off with pride, lived in it, despite all the dirt.

When I finished rallying and moved away from the scene, my cut-off continued to reside in the wardrobe. Throughout my time at university, marrying and buying a house the cut-off remained. A touchstone of my youth; proof of a rite of passage. It hung there as a reminder of a previous life, more tangible than any photograph could possibly be. Looking at each badge brought back a different weekend, a different journey. Feeling the material and closing my eyes, I could recall the rides in detail – the speed, the adrenaline, the beautifully taken corners and the painful mistakes. Real, visceral memory.

One day I noticed it had gone from the wardrobe. I asked my then wife where it was, thinking it may have been moved to the garage, or worse, the loft. I felt real shock and anger when she told me she had thrown it out because it was dirty and smelled. How could she do such a thing? How could she be so insensitive? To me it showed a clear disregard for who I once was. Still was. Would be again. I was truly hurt.

I still have a denim jacket. A Levi, of course. It isn't torn or faded, and is regularly washed. A black denim jacket, perhaps more sedate or mature? It carries no badge, other than its own, and for me, today, this is enough. As with any item of clothing, it says something about me, although it says it quietly compared to the jackets of my youth.

© Paul Atkinson 2008

JEANS:

From work-wear to the designer showroom

Jeans began to be a significant symbol of rebellious youth from the 1950's onwards, but their associations with radicalism date back to the French Revolution. The story of jeans is enmeshed within working class cultures where they were valued for their affordability, strength and practicality, qualities that attracted affluent non-conformists such as Lord Byron, the poet and freedom fighter of the early 19th century, who adopted sailor's wide white duck trousers for daywear and workman's narrow black jean trousers for eveningwear. Byron's message was clear – it was cool to imitate the working classes.

By the 19th century, denim jeans were essential for American miners, loggers, farmers, and labourers. The durability of the denim accommodated much patching and mending, a necessity when money was scarce and replacement expensive. Practicality dominated over style – typically, jeans had lots of pockets for tools and visible double stitching strengthened the seams.

Jeans for work-wear continued to gain ground in the early 20th century, but it was the emergence of a new film genre – the cowboy films of the 1930's and '40's – that reinforced romantic associations between jeans, rugged masculinity and the introverted male as hero. This trend continued to develop through the 1950's, headed by Marlon Brando and James Dean, both of whom wore jeans in their most famous screen roles. Towards the end of the '50's, young American city-dwelling blacks who emulated these role models took to wearing jeans – the very symbol of their fathers' and grandfathers' exploitation in the cotton fields – but modified them to make them 'cool', so cool that they were adopted by

British Mods in the 60's. Sub-cultural modification had eliminated all reference to work-wear – these jeans were pristine, carefully pressed, and altered to fit perfectly. In a word, they were sharp.

Throughout the 1960's, American jeans increased their influence on European fashion but were difficult to obtain, particularly for women who preferred the androgynous jeans cut to the prevailing curvaceous 'slacks' silhouette. Doris Day-style curves were out; the French, gamine look, was in. The unisexual practice of wearing new jeans in a warm bath to obtain the perfect fit implanted the trend for customizing the mass-produced, and Levi's became the largest manufacturers of jeans in the world. The popularity of jeans increased apace with availability. By the 1970's jeans had achieved the status of radical chic and satisfied the desire for modern individualism. Although many people wear jeans a lot of the time, the more a pair of jeans are worn, the more they become personalized through individual patterns of wear.

By the 1980's it was apparent that jeans had become mainstream. Marks and Spencer collaborated in 1984 with the Fashion department of the Royal College of Art to design a range of women's jeans that combined toughness with femininity (below).

Today, growing commitment to recycling has inspired the alchemy of transforming worn denim into an art form, as seen in the work of ex-Levi's creative director, Gary Harvey, who reconfigured 42 pairs of worn jeans (left) and 28 camouflage jackets (right) into a powerful pastiche of the catwalk look.

Small designer labels are increasing; the desire for vintage jeans is mounting, and the luxury of the bespoke beckons. In response to the consumer swing away from mass production, Levi stores offer scanning technology to achieve the perfect fit with personalised design details; other companies will etch the customer's own laser designs and signatures into the fabric, or weave jean lengths on antique Japanese looms. Chanel's 2006 disjunction of a jewel-encrusted dress with jeans (below) resonates with Byron's duck trousers and finely-tailored coat. These developments highlight the competitive edge to wearing denim, and remove it far from the idealistic, anti-materialist, non-conformity of the mid 20th century. Jeans have come a long way from the mines and forests of America

I'M THINKING ABOUT

One thing that interests me about denim is its relationship to ideas of the outsider – it's status as a garment of social opposition.

Denim functions as a type of *'armour'* (Eco) and as an ultimately personal garment,a second skin, one that speaks of the passage of time and the interaction with the wearer.

I'm thinking about...I'm writing about why we wear our pants so low, you know, dope style, looking the bomb when you're bustin slack...

We obsess over keeping it real (Don't we?) I mean- its so , yknow, that thing of really having been there, having to be there... I mean. We can now buy trademarked 'cool' off the shelf and that power to buy that need to be more authentic [1], the need to keep it real creates, apart from a whole lot of things it creates all kinds of niche markets ...

(I'm thinking of *'Rockin' my Dickies*..or ...*My Adidas*)...)

– one of the niche markets is the trade in prison clothing...an ultimate outsider lifestyle whose garments can be worn like a badge of commodified dissent or disaffection on the street and traded up. And this, apparently, is the reason why certain zealous Sheriffs are dying prison uniforms pink, to defeat this illicit trade, especially the underwear; pink jockeys, pink boxers... and some are doing the jail cells too...pink bars and pink walls - a delirious frenzy of shocking schiaperelli ... there's a photo of Mike Tyson in pink bracelets and pink slippers...the idea being to humiliate the wearer, remove the machismo braggadocio of the whole jailin' thing...of course, I'm fascinated by this, because I get fascinated by the minutiae of microfashion...like that gang thing a couple of years ago, in NY, wearing sponge hair rollers threaded into the laces of your trainers...or the must-have accessory of a plastic rainhood, hang it from your key fob when you're double saggin' to really look the bomb...but I digress..

The more I check this, the more I discover that like so many ideas about outsiderness or counter culturalism, it shapeshifts as I try to touch it...it goes in and out of focus.

For a start...the Prison Blues...the idea that there are prison issue denims...they haven't really been around in America since the late thirties, around the time the dude ranches [2] were taking off. Back then so many people were in debt and in jail for it that you could wear your work clothes inside. The governors weren't in a very nasty mood. 'Poverty is a great equaliser' [3]. Prison Uniform tends to reflect the anger of society ...it's punitive mood - right now there's an absolute bonanza of punitiveness. The prisons are fit to bust and - zebra stripes are replacing the orange 'pumpkin' jumpsuits - like the old 'I Was a Fugitive from a Chain Gang' look from the 30s and Sheriffs are madder than ever and meanwhile in northern Oregon they're making prisoners make 'Prison Blues' workwear to sell on the outside - very popular with loggers and bikers according to the testimonials - and the whole thing comes full circle. Least ways it appears to until I begin to investigate colour - thinking about pink and blue and I discover that blue was associated with women and pink with boys. Its a mixed up muddled up shook up world (except for Lola). Blue for the Virgin Mary (and therefore pale blue for little girls) and red for valour, strength (qualities attributed to the 'male') and therefore a lesser red : pink, for boys. [4]That's why the Nazi's had pink triangles to demark men who liked men and that how, gradually, it all got swapped around last century, and it is sooo last century, because actually the mad-as-hell Sheriffs discovered that pink has such a calming effect that its good for guys on the inside - it's the right colour to chill and ill to....now we can all kick back with pink...pink peg slacks , just like Eddie...oh I digress.....I meant to write about saggin ; wearing your jeans (or your Dickies) so low like that ....and how word was, on the street, that was down, down with the brothers on the inside...but really that's another myth, or a least a little shapeshift...a little mythos but I'll put that in another footnote somewhere further on ...FURTHUR;)

further: the legend and history of saggin and bustin'

Here is a confession, (even if confession is overrated) : my name is x and I'm addicted to denim. I could quit anytime but why should I want to? I've been scouring the streets for too long now, since the early nineties to be exact, ok, it goes back further...much further. I'd like several decades to be taken into account if truth be [5]...but let's focus on the discovery of Japanese denim...early 90s, hanging out in Slam City and I see this guy in jeans like I haven't seen, least since I found that dead stock of big E's in '76, but I do digress. And I ask him, I say 'Where dya get them?' ' Japan?' I had heard there was a buzz about Japanese Lee Riders and something goes click in my head, and later, maybe a year or so, in a little shop near there called PIL they have some Evis jeans...and the weight, the styling, the obsessive detail of these jeans is singular and so different::::so appealing::::

Now, I was wearing early Holmes, if memory serves, Zoo York and Subware at the time, sizing up and, naturally, saggin' my pants. For the record, sizing up, going baggy, started in the 80s [6], a converse trend to the downsized silhouette starved-to-near-perfection look of the seventies. The popularity and rightness of the Agbada (Yoruba) or Yogi Pants, Kurtas and Dhotis and their influence and their gradual incorporation into mainstream fashion during that time [7] all added to that bigger, looser, look. It had been coming a long time.

sub-culture [8]/mainstream stop making sense:

If there needs to be any explanation for anything in fashion - because at the time skaters were up sizing from 30" or 32" to 38" or 40" - it just couldn't get any bigger and t-shirts were worn XXL at least. No one had any explanation. This is a moment (early 90s) when Vans were just about unavailable, skaters had 'gone out of fashion in the 80s' as far as most people were concerned and the understanding of Dogtown and Z-Boys (in Britain) was limited to about a room full of people, mostly (young(ish)) men. Skating and Graf were the last of the tribal cultures to be commodified (and how they got commodified!) But denim wasn't that crucial. Jeans came in all kinds of colours (think MC Hammer) and indigo was just one. Then along came Evis and suddenly all that fifties, even forties, certainly sixties stuff bit back and the look changed. Again, only for a handful of people but it was crucial now...and cued in, from about '95, the catwalk breakout of denim that hit in 2000 and continues to the present in both the High Street and the 'Premium Denim' market.

There are microfashions within microfashions and for some it gets very detailed...but you could focus down on an acre of ground between Neals Yard and Earlam Street where a lot of this happened. Between Slam City Skates and American Classics.

'Last night a blogspot saved my life.

There is a world where rivets, doughnuts, fades, the names of different types of fades; the whiskers, honeycombs and breaks, have a particular resonance: Electro c'est ma life. Denim is Love: 'maybe you wouldn't understand but the love for denim is something unexplainable. the fades, whiskers, honeycombs, breaks. ahhhh... denim is truly love.'"
minou-prod.blogspot.com

The appreciation of this minutiae is documented, shared, relayed and responded to. It bounces around the globe, from Japan to Sweden, from Kyoto to York, Paris to... from artists and aficionados there is a carnival of denim that parades 24/7, guys in jeans going for the fade, don't wash till Hammersmith, take a look at Erik's pages; compare and contrast the effect of leaving a Studio D'Artisan wallet in the back pocket of a pair of Samurai SO500XX and wearing them for eight months without washing-see Erik's labour of love of all things denim repeattofade.com or read Paul T's threads on Superfuture Supertalk Superdenim or ...start your own.

Why denim? Because...because it speaks, tells it's tale, provides a narrative, implies a history, imparts meaning, bears the tracks and traces, stains and memories of its passage; it is a marker of time.

Footnotes

1/ Of course, commodification of the cool has altered function and any notions of authenticity and origin are cut loose from meaning.

2/ Denim first became (widely) popular in the States as a 'play' garment when East Coast holiday makers travelled west to experience the nostalgic otherness of a cattle ranch. A cheap holiday in someone else's misery. Dude ranches; real ranches, hit by the Depression, transformed into playgrounds of cowboy lifestyle...the 'cowboy' - a cinematic creation - the term had originally been used by ranchers to denote the black American rounders and cattle men or 'boys' as they were pejoratively called. A celluloid signifier onto which images of rugged individualism and the tatters of the American Dream could be fitted. Meanwhile...dustbowl faces were being immortalised by Walker Evans into images of romantic poverty...poverty porno...in denim overalls...cool looks that collegiates in northern California would pick up on in the late thirties and get banned from school for wearing waisted overalls....

3/ During the Depression, hordes of people wound up in prison for petty crimes, vagrancy and debt. "Everyone was poor. That was a great equalizer," Levin said. "The idea of who was a criminal changed." Sheriffs started issuing work shirts and jeans. Some lockups let inmates wear their own clothes because the jails couldn't afford uniforms.

Denim gave way to khaki in the 1940s, then to solid-color cotton scrubs. Road crews started wearing orange jumpsuits so they'd be easy to spot. Professor Jack Levin, Northeastern University, Boston.

4/ Koller,Veronika(forthcoming 2009): "'More than just a colour': pink as a gender and sexuality marker in visual communication". Visual Communication, 8.1/2.

5/ From my own relationship with denim I begin in the 60s - Mods in coveted, rare '66 501s...Denim's appropriation by successive groups of sub cultural minorities as a signifier of liminality was so firmly entrenched during that period that by the mid 70s it was recouped into the mainstream...and post-punk provocateurs marked themselves out by not wearing the cloth. Picture Ian Curtis in jeans? Actually, its role always has been one of recouperation and the line between 'mainstream' and it's opposite now seems blurred and denim has slipped in and out of its different roles and meanings.

6/ unless you start to consider the Zoot Suit and that is a whole different story

7/ 'Sagging is commonly assumed to have originated in the prohibition of belts among incarcerated inmates, when belts were confiscated to prevent prisoners hanging themselves. It has also been rumored that Sagging while incarcerated means that the inmate is "available". The fashion statement eventually spread to urban youth. However, such a statement, report or belief is subjective and carries racist overtones; connecting urban or hip hop culture to criminals or prisoners when in reality "prisoners" in Southern California(like most prisoners) wear (orange) jumpsuits which are an all in one outfits i.e. void of any place to even place a belt—next, it is more evident that it started on the streets and (like most cultures) was brought into the prison and not vise-versa according to a report by National Public Radio (NPR) (2006) "They are issued a jumpsuit, but in two days at the facility, there doesn't seem to be a single prisoner wearing one. All of them are wearing their underwear, white boxer shorts, t-shirts and flip-flops" (NPR, 2006,Monitor.Control.Isolate section, ¶5) Aaron, Yahoo.

Also, it is suggested that the trends are said to initially be worn by Southern California gang members, it became popular when gangsta rap artists from Los Angeles became popular in the early 90s and was also called "bustin' slack." However, baggy pants or as it is popularily refered to as sagging (which is baggy looking but with under-garments exposed) really have their origins in eastern culture i.e. people in Africa, Asia and many indigenous people wore and some continue to wear loose-fitting or saggy style clothes. Aaron. Yahoo

- -

8/ ...And, of course, New Romanticism (which meant never having to say you were sorry) and the Hard Times/Rockabilly look that followed/ran parallel meant...future-retro...and Morrissey fans in 501s from Strangeways to Echo Park; cholos and pachucos in quiffs like Billy Fury and... you realise this comes around and around- the exchange, appropriation and cross sub-cultural hybridisation of ways of wearing, cutting a style, dressing for carnivale...where the world turns upside down.

© Richard Knight 2008

SONG TO DENIM

(WITH APOLOGISES TO VAN MORRISON)

In the days before denim
No rock and roll
In the days before rock and roll
Silence
In the silence
Longing
In the days before denim
Drab wet fifties streets
In the days before Elvis
No blue jeans
In the days before rock and roll
Just school
In the days before life began
Parents
In the days before the Stones
Alma Cogan
In the days before denim
Cavalry Twill
Then the world began, well, mine did then
Sitting on the cross with my pushbike chatting up the birds

In the days before rock and roll
I couldn't have been Elvis
In the days before denim
No quiff
In the days before rock and roll
No DA
In the days before denim
No blue striped T-shirt
In the days before rock and roll
No denims
In the days before denim
No sex
In the days before rock and roll
No Radio Luxemburg
In the days before denim
No proper shoes
In the days before rock and roll
No girls
Then the world began, well, mine did then
Sitting on my life waiting for the world to chat me up

In the days before denim
Alone
In the days before rock and roll
Their god
In the days before denim
Sundays in the rain
In the days before rock and roll
No Gene Vincent
On all the days before denim
Longing
In the days before rock and roll
Sunday School
In the days before denim
No rock and roll
No rock and roll
In the days of rock and roll
In the days of rock and roll
Oh
In the days
After
Rock and roll
Still denim
Then, after the world had begun, as mine had then
With the world waiting for me to chat it up

There is
Still rock and roll
Still denim
Like the man said
Do not go quietly
Still denim
Still rock and roll

Now, sitting on my life
After the world has chatted me up
Always denim
Always rock and roll

© *Phil Cosker 2008*